Questioning the Author

Comprehension Guide
Grade 4

Harcourt School Publishers

www.harcourtschool.com

Printed in the United States of America

ISBN 10 0-15-359241-9

ISBN 13 978-0-15-359241-6

4 5 6 7 8 9 10 082 16 15 14 13 12 11 10 09 08

Contents

The Hot and Cold Summer 2

Mighty Jackie: The Strike-Out Queen 4

Danitra Brown Leaves Town 6

Kai's Journey to Gold Mountain 8

On the Banks of Plum Creek 10

Justin and the Best Biscuits in the World 12

Three Little Cyberpigs 14

Weaving a California Tradition 16

Mimicry and Camouflage 18

Mountains 20

Fire Storm 22

The Stranger 24

So You Want to Be an Inventor? 26

Just Like Me 28

Hewitt Anderson's Great Big Life 30

Juan Verdades: The Man Who Couldn't Tell a Lie 32

Because of Winn-Dixie 34

My Diary from Here to There 36

The Cricket in Times Square 38

Mangrove Wilderness 40

Dragons and Dinosaurs 42

Grand Canyon: A Trail Through Time 44

The Bunyans 46

John Muir and Stickeen 48

Introduction

Questioning the Author (QtA) *Comprehension Guide* provides an alternative format for guiding students' comprehension as they read a text selection. By using the sequence of questions in QtA, teachers can support their students in thinking about and understanding what they read. The QtA questions target important events and ideas in a text and assist students in making connections among them.

How QtA Was Developed

The QtA approach was developed by Drs. Isabel Beck and Margaret McKeown (Beck & McKeown, 2006; McKeown, Beck, & Worthy, 1993) in response to their earlier research (Beck, McKeown, Sinatra, & Loxterman, 1991; McKeown & Beck, 1990) that showed that, all too often, students simply skimmed the surface of text and could answer only questions that required them to repeat text information. QtA was designed to encourage students to dig below the surface of text so that they really understand the ideas. The following are the three central features of QtA:

QtA takes place during the initial reading of a text. Students alternate between reading a portion of text and discussing the ideas they encounter in it. As text is read, the teacher stops the reading at certain points and poses questions to initiate discussion. In the lesson plans that follow—📖—identifies a line from the selection as the place to stop and pose the numbered question. This alternating of reading and discussion illustrates to students that building meaning from text is an iterative process in which ideas are considered as they are offered. Through this process, students come to understand that a good reader does not move steadily through the words of a text until the end is reached and only then begin to think about what was read.

QtA begins with the teacher posing general, open-ended questions whose goal is students' comprehension of the material. The questions that are provided in this guide tap central text events and ideas and their interrelationships. The sequence of questions tracks the progression of ideas and events in the text. The QtA questions signal students to consider the ideas being expressed, and the questions support them in putting these ideas together into a meaningful representation of the text content.

Typical QtA initiating queries are:

- What is the author trying to say?
- What is the author's message?
- What does the author want us to know?
- What is the author setting up?
- What's happening here?

QtA encourages discussion in which students are invited to grapple with ideas in order to construct meaning. Students listen to their peers' ideas and respond with contributions that promote collaborative development of understanding. The teacher's role in the discussion is to follow up on students' initial responses, prompting students to elaborate on and extend their thinking while being careful not to take over the thinking for students.

Asking open-ended questions makes it possible for students to respond in a variety of ways. What they say may be sparse; their responses may simply reiterate words from the text without addressing meaning; or their responses may indicate misunderstanding. In these situations, the teacher needs to follow up with questions, such as

- What do you think that means?
- How do the last [two] lines we just read connect to what we already know?
- What did we read that explains that situation?
- What does the conversation between [two characters] tell us about their relationship?
- How does this add to what we already know about [a character]?

As students' initial responses are followed up, meaning is built through interactive discussion.

Why QtA Works

Through practice with interspersed QtA questions, students are taught to address text ideas while they are reading. This process of pausing to think about the content they have just read mimics the manner in which proficient readers build meaning during reading. As students take on text little by little and respond to well-placed questions, they become accustomed to discussing ideas in order to make sense of what they are reading.

What Research Has Shown About QtA

Research on QtA showed significant changes in classroom discourse about text (Beck, McKeown, Worthy, Sandora, & Kucan, 1996; McKeown, Beck, & Sandora, 1996). When QtA was used, talk about text focused on ideas from the text, what the ideas mean, and how they connect, rather than on retrieving information directly from the text. Students were much more active participants in discussions, talking between two and three times as much as before. They phrased their contributions in their own words and drew connections between ideas. Students were also much more likely to initiate their own questions and comments and to interact explicitly with the comments of other students. In addition, the study of individual student comprehension suggests that QtA students showed better monitoring of comprehension—that is, they could identify where they were having trouble comprehending a text passage (McKeown & Beck, 1998).

References

Beck, I. L., & McKeown, M. G. *Improving Comprehension with Questioning the Author: A Fresh and Enhanced View of a Proven Approach*. New York: Scholastic, Inc. 2006.

Beck, I. L., McKeown, M. G., Sinatra, G. M., & Loxterman, J. A. "Revising social studies text from a text-processing perspective: Evidence of improved comprehensibility." In *Reading Research Quarterly*, 26, pp. 251–276. 1991.

Beck, I. L., McKeown, M. G., Worthy, J., Sandora, C., & Kucan, L. "Questioning the Author: A Yearlong Classroom Implementation to Engage Students with Text." In *Elementary School Journal,* 96.4, pp. 385–414. 1996.

McKeown, M. G., & Beck, I. L. "The assessment and characterization of young learners' knowledge of a topic in history." In *American Educational Research Journal*, 27, pp. 688–726. 1990.

McKeown, M. G., & Beck, I. L. "Talking to an author: Readers taking charge of the reading process." In R. Calfee & N. Nelson (eds.), "The reading-writing connection." *Ninety-seventh yearbook for the National Society for the Study of Education* (pp. 112–130). Chicago: National Society for the Study of Education. 1998.

McKeown, M. G., Beck, I. L., and Sandora, C. A. "Questioning the Author: An approach to developing meaningful classroom discourse." In Graves, M. G., Taylor, B. M., & van den Broek, P. *The first R: Every child's right to read*. Teachers College Press (pp. 97–119). 1996 (Reprinted in *Reading Research Anthology: The Why? of Reading Instruction: Consortium on Reading Excellence* (pp. 156–178). CA: Arena Press. 1999.)

McKeown, M. G., Beck, I. L., & Worthy, M. J. "Grappling with text ideas: Questioning the Author." *In The Reading Teacher*, 46, pp. 560–566. 1993.

The Hot and Cold Summer,
pages 26–40

📖 **Will the three of them be able to stay friends?**

1. To establish what happened in the novel before this excerpt: **What is the author letting us know about the characters?** (Possible response: At first Rory and Derek refused to befriend Bolivia. Now both boys are friends with her, but Derek has spent part of the summer away at camp.)

FOLLOW-UP: **What does the way the boys befriended Bolivia tell you about them?** (Possible response: Maybe they're hard to get to know, because each needed time to get to know Bolivia without the other around.)

📖 **Or maybe he . . . need Rory anymore.**

2. To establish that Rory is concerned about the state of his friendship with Derek: **What's going on with Rory?** (Possible response: He's nervous about Derek returning from camp because they argued before he left.)

📖 **Probably now that . . . rest his toes.**

3. To further highlight Rory's personality: **What's going on now?** (Possible response: Rory is thinking about all the ways his actions affected his friendship with Derek and Bolivia.)

FOLLOW-UP: **How does this add to what we know about Rory so far?** (Possible response: He can't stop agonizing over his life and the people in it.)

📖 **"And, besides, I . . . at camp."**

4. To understand that Derek is much too caring to hold a grudge: **What's the author telling us about Derek now?** (Possible response: He's super-nice—by his giving up swimming and by his bringing comics to Rory, we see he's not holding a grudge against Rory for their argument before camp.)

📖 **Bolivia said . . . opened Lucette's cage.**

5. To determine that the three friends are getting along beautifully and that Rory wasted a lot of time worrying: **What does this conversation show us about the three friends?** (Possible response: There isn't any tension between them, as Rory had worried there would be.)

📖 **"If we had two pies . . . do it."**

6. To establish that the author is having Bolivia and Rory side with each other against Derek—that Bolivia and Rory have become close friends: **What's the author showing us about the three friends with this conversation?** (Possible response: The author wants us to see that Bolivia and Rory have forged a strong relationship over the summer, so she has them side against Derek.)

FOLLOW-UP: **What does the mood of the conversation tell us about the friends?** (Possible response: That although they're competitive, they aren't mean-spirited.)

📖 **"I'll tell them to deliver . . . eating here."**

7. To elicit that Bolivia is so sure neither boy can eat a whole pizza that she'll risk hard-earned money and getting no pizza to prove it: **What does Bolivia think of this competition?** *(Possible response: She's so sure the boys will leave pizza for her to eat that she offers their lemonade money for the second pizza.)*

📖 **"I'll bring it inside to her," promised Bolivia.**

8. To further emphasize that Bolivia is convinced the boys are wrong: **What's Bolivia saying about the competition when she promises to bring extra pizza in for Edna?** *(Possible response: There's no way either boy can win—there will be extra slices for sure.)*

📖 **Unfortunately, it . . . imagined it would.**

9. To draw attention to the way Rory is feeling during the competition: **What does it mean when Rory thinks, "unfortunately, it didn't taste quite as good as he had imagined it would"?** *(Possible response: He's getting so full that having the chance to eat as much pizza as possible has resulted in its not tasting as good as he imagined it would.)*

📖 **"You worked hard selling the lemonade."**

10. To establish that Derek and Rory are both starting to pull out of the competition and Bolivia is making it hard for them: **What's all this talk of fairness about?** *(Possible response: Both boys are trying to get Bolivia to take a slice of pizza by saying she's entitled to it and Bolivia's refusing to let them off the hook.)*

📖 **"I'm having a . . . slices together.**

11. To establish that Bolivia was right about the boys: **What's going on here?** *(Possible response: Bolivia has accepted a slice of pizza from each boy and has proven they couldn't eat a whole pizza.)*

📖 **Neither had any room at all.**

12. To clarify that Bolivia saw herself as part of the competition: **What's happening?** *(Possible response: Bolivia has announced that there is a three-way tie in the competition.)*
FOLLOW-UP: **What do the boys think of her announcement?** *(Possible response: They don't agree, because she didn't eat her crusts.)*

📖 **It was great . . . Derek and Bolivia.**

13. To establish that despite Rory's current limitations, he is very lucky to have such good friends: **How does the way Rory feels now connect to the way he felt in the beginning of the story?** *(Possible response: He is satisfied that he and his friends will be able to get along. He feels good.)*

page 60

📖 Jackie was young . . . major league baseball.

1. To set up that a girl pitching a baseball game against the New York Yankees in 1931 was extraordinary: **What has the author told us about April 2, 1931?** (*Possible response: The famous Yankees were playing an exhibition game against a team that featured a female pitcher.*)

page 62

📖 Or that's what they thought.

2. To establish the patronizing tone of the media and townspeople toward Jackie playing baseball: **What did everyone think about Jackie playing baseball?** (*Possible response: People were rude, comparing her to a trained seal and telling her girls weren't supposed to play baseball. Using the statement "you throw like a girl" would have been the ultimate insult to a boy.*)

page 63

📖 She worked hard.

3. To understand that Jackie had men in her life that believed she was a capable baseball player: **How does what Jackie's father and the baseball player, Dazzy Vance, think of her connect to what everyone else seems to think?** (*Possible response: They believe in her talents, encourage her, and coach her in how to be a great baseball player.*)

📖 But it didn't . . . her arm knew.

4. To begin to develop the idea of Jackie's high level of dedication: **What does Jackie's throwing until she couldn't see tell you about**

her? (*Possible response: She wants to be a great pitcher so badly that she'll practice until she's exhausted.*)

page 64

📖 Jackie was ready . . . her left hand.

5. To establish that despite the huge crowd, everyone expecting her to fail, and playing against famous big-leaguers, Jackie is confident—prepared to perform: **What do Jackie's thoughts tell us about the kind of person she is?** (*Possible response: She's brave and ready to play despite the odds against her.*)

📖 "It would kill . . . ball every day."

6. To solidify Babe Ruth's attitude toward females and baseball: **What does Babe Ruth think about girls and baseball?** (*Possible response: He doesn't think they're strong enough to play.*)
FOLLOW-UP: **How do Babe's thoughts about girls connect to Dazzy Vance's?** (*Possible response: Both are professional players, but Babe doesn't have the same belief in females that Dazzy does. Dazzy seems like a nicer person.*)

page 67

📖 "STRRRRIKE TWO!"

7. To highlight the way Jackie's self-talk and her ability to block out the crowd allows her to perform the way she wants to: **How does the way Jackie talks to herself affect the way she pitches?** (*Possible response: She's coaching herself into believing she can strike out the best hitter in baseball, and she's doing it.*)

© Harcourt

FOLLOW-UP: **What's Babe Ruth thinking about the game so far?** (*Possible response: He's not too pleased.*)

page 68

📖 **What would the papers say tomorrow?**

8. To establish that Jackie has struck out the best hitter in baseball and Babe is behaving like a fragile child: **What's going on?** (*Possible response: Jackie has done the impossible— struck out the "Sultan of Swat.")*

FOLLOW-UP: **How is Babe Ruth handling his strikeout?** (*Possible response: He's acting like a spoiled child, saying he'll never hit against a woman again.*)

📖 **"STRRRRIKE THREE!"**

9. To solidify the great amount of confidence Jackie is feeling: **Why was Jackie grinning in what must have been a very stressful moment in her life?** (*Possible response: She knew her hard work was paying off with every good pitch she threw.*)

page 70

📖 **She'd shown the . . . as she wanted.**

10. To focus on the crowd's change in attitude toward Jackie: **What has Jackie's pitching done to the crowd?** (*Possible response: They adore her now. They're cheering her on, thrilled to have seen what she could do.*)

To further demonstrate Jackie's unwillingness to let the crowd determine whether she feels good or bad: **How does Jackie's lukewarm reaction to the crowd suddenly supporting her connect to the way the crowd affected her when they booed?** (*Possible response: She's so confident and proud of her abilities that the crowd cheering or jeering doesn't seem to matter much to her.*)

Danitra Brown Leaves Town, pages 84–98

page 86

📖 **School is out . . . one afternoon.**

1. To establish that the story will probably be about Danitra's summer vacation: **What's the author letting us know with this one sentence?** *(Possible response: This story looks to be about someone named Danitra—someone who clearly loves summer and all that it means to her.)*

page 87

📖 **But why am . . . and loving it?**

2. To have students discern that the narrator is unhappy that Danitra's going on vacation: **What's the narrator letting us know about herself when she says, "But why am I supposed to care when my supposed-to-be best friend is leaving me, and loving it?"** *(Possible response: She's not able to be happy for Danitra's vacation.)*

page 88

📖 **Maybe the summer wouldn't be such . . . a bore.**

3. To have students recognize that the narrator has found a new friend—a girl she never paid attention to before: **What's going on?** *(Possible response: The narrator has made friends with Nina, someone she never noticed before.)*

page 89

📖 **I wish that you were here.**

4. To establish how important it was for Zuri to know Danitra missed her and wasn't mad: **Why was it so important for Zuri to read the words "I wish that you were here"?** *(Possible*

response: Zuri was nervous that Danitra would still be mad at the way she treated Danitra right before she left for vacation. Those words show Danitra isn't mad.)*

page 91

📖 **In a blink . . . fancy-dancing fool.**

5. To have students consider what Danitra and Zuri's letters show about their summer experiences: **What do the two letters show us about each of the girls' summers so far?** *(Possible response: Danitra's summer seems peaceful and quiet so far, while Zuri's seems full of energy and clamor.)*

page 93

📖 **He can't, and that's a fact.**

6. To have students recognize both girls are facing and overcoming problems in their own ways: **What have we learned from these two letters?** *(Possible response: Both girls have faced uncomfortable situations and overcome them using cleverness and/or skill to show they are confident and capable.)*

page 95

📖 **The holiday seemed . . . late-night fire-works.**

7. To establish that Zuri seems to find comfort and peace in spending the Fourth of July with her mother—seeing her mom laugh and act like a kid: **What does this letter show us about Zuri and her mom?** *(Possible response: The Fourth of July was a special opportunity for them to be together, both acting like kids, enjoying each moment of the day.)*

📖 I am part of a family.

8. To highlight the way Danitra found comfort and enjoyment in spending her Fourth of July with a lot of relatives—she liked being part of a big family gathering: **What does Danitra's letter show us about her Fourth of July?** *(Possible response: She had a good time, feeling the love of a large family—making her feel connected and special.)*

To have students determine the way each had a Fourth of July experience that seemed to fill a need: **What do the experiences of both girls show us about what they needed in their lives?** *(Possible response: Each girl had a great Fourth of July, even though their days were very different. Zuri seemed to need special time with her mom, while Danitra seemed to need the love of many people.)*

📖 A good hello . . . times better.

9. To establish that the last line of the story seems to indicate that although the girls were apart, their friendship is stronger than ever: **How have things finished up for Danitra and Zuri?** *(Possible response: This last sentence shows us that Danitra and Zuri have probably grown even closer by having spent the summer apart.)*

To have students consider the way Danitra's summer advice (first page of story) measures up with the reality of her summer: **Thinking back to the list of things Danitra advised for summer vacation, how do you think her summer measured up?** *(Possible response: Although she didn't do the items on the list, she seemed very happy with her summer experiences.)*

Kai's Journey to Gold Mountain, pages 112–127

📖 **After a long night . . . strange, new place.**

1. To have students discern that Kai, who is traveling to America after his father has summoned him through a letter, is uneasy about his lonely journey and about some questions he will soon have to answer: **What's the author letting us know about Kai?** *(Possible response: He seems brave for someone so young. After receiving a letter from his father, he is traveling to the United States alone and is worried about some upcoming questions he will have to answer.)*

📖 **Instead he found . . . pointy wire.**

2. To establish Kai's kind nature and that the island seems prison-like: **What's the author showing us with her description of Kai's morning?** *(Possible response: It seems more like jail—guards, everyone being corralled, bad food, high metal fence—than a stopping point for immigrants.)*
FOLLOW-UP: **What does the author show us about Kai when he tries not to disturb the old man sleeping below him?** *(Possible response: He's considerate, even with people he doesn't know.)*

📖 **Kai suspected that . . . back to China.**

3. To connect Kai's earlier worries about answering questions to his observations that some of the immigrants were released into San Francisco and some were not: **How does the fact that some people are released to San Francisco and some are sent back to China connect to Kai's worries about being questioned?** *(Possible response: The way people answer the questions seems to determine whether they are released into America.)*

📖 **Kai dragged his . . . terribly alone.**

4. To draw attention to the depressing wait all the men and boys experience: **How does the old man's poem fit with Kai's experience on the island?** *(Possible response: The poem conveys a sense of sadness, and Kai seems depressed and anxious about his current situation.)*

📖 **"There must be a way. . . . "**

5. To highlight that Kai is working on a plan involving plums: **What's Kai up to?** *(Possible response: He seems to be trying to come up with a way to get some plums that are growing outside the fence.)*

📖 **Sticky juice ran . . . laughed and laughed.**

6. To have students examine the way the boys react to eating the plums: **Why are the plums so important to the boys?** *(Possible response: After countless days eating bland, repetitive meals, the plums taste especially scrumptious.)*

© Harcourt

page 120

📖 "Don't give up on me, Father," . . . his pillow.

7. To have students consider the great importance of the letter from Kai's father: **Why does Kai finger his letter each night?** *(Possible response: The letter is the one thing connecting him to his father at this time. It's reassuring to him—like a security blanket.)*

page 121

📖 A white woman . . . men spoke.

8. To establish that Kai's interrogation is going well: **What's going on?** *(Possible response: Kai is being questioned and things are going well.)*

page 122

📖 "That's not what your father said."

9. To clarify that the questioning has turned to intricate details that for some reason Kai seems to get wrong: **What's all this about chairs?** *(Possible response: It seems as though the interrogators are trying to trick Kai.)* To establish that Kai must be very upset with his situation: **Knowing what we do about Kai, what might he be thinking?** *(Possible response: This is what he'd been afraid of since he got to the island.)*

page 123

📖 Kai didn't dare smile . . . over him.

10. To determine that Kai's boldness paid off: **How did Kai handle the rest of the interrogation?** *(Possible response: He took a chance by explaining why his answer might have been different from his father's and the men were impressed. Kai feels pleased with the interrogators' responses.)*

page 125

📖 He turned to the open door . . . the sunshine.

11. To draw attention to Kai's mixed emotions: **How does Kai scrambling down from the top bunk and his knees shaking with joy connect to his solemn bows and soft words to Young?** *(Possible response: He's thrilled to finally go to his father, but he shows respect for his friend's sad feelings.)*

page 126

📖 Shuddering at the . . . interrogation room.

12. To further accentuate Kai's kind nature: **What does it tell us that Kai is still concerned about leaving Young behind?** *(Possible response: He's a caring person, always thinking of others.)*

page 127

📖 And as they stood . . . Gold Mountain.

13. To establish that finding Gold Mountain meant being with his father as much as gaining entrance to America: **What did Kai mean when he said he'd found Gold Mountain?** *(Possible response: Being with his father is what gives him the feeling of safety and contentment as much as having his feet on American soil.)*

On the Banks of
Plum Creek, pages 158–169

page 160

📖 **Mary was going . . . were gone.**

1. To establish some characteristics of prairie life: **What has the author set up for us so far?** *(Possible response: Laura's family is getting ready for winter.)*
FOLLOW-UP: **What does it tell us that Pa and Ma leave Laura and Mary to take care of the house while they go into town?** *(Possible response: Ma and Pa trust that the girls are responsible.)*

📖 **Ma wore her hoopskirts . . . Big Woods.**

2. To solidify that going into town was a big deal: **What's going on?** *(Possible response: Ma and Carrie are getting dressed up.)*
FOLLOW-UP: **What does this tell us about the trip?** *(Possible response: The way they're dressing shows how special the trip to town is for the family.)*

page 161

📖 **They washed their . . . them away.**

3. To elicit that so far the girls are having fun, though they keep their fun within safe limits: **What are the girls up to?** *(Possible response: The girls are playing and having their lunch.)*
FOLLOW-UP: **What does it tell us that they did not go near the swimming hole and did not touch the straw stack?** *(Possible response: It seems as though they've been told not to do those things, and they didn't. They're good girls.)*

page 162

📖 **"I guess I can play where I want to!"**

4. To establish that Laura has a strong personality: **What's going on between Laura and Mary?** *(Possible response: They're arguing about playing on the big rock.)*
FOLLOW-UP: **What does this argument show us about Laura?** *(Possible response: Laura is determined to do what she wants even if her older sister tells her not to.)*

📖 **Pa was not there . . . cattle away.**

5. To establish that Laura and Mary are now responsible for fixing a big problem: **What's going on with the cattle and the hay?** *(Possible response: A herd of cattle have begun to eat and pick apart the stacks of hay that the family needs to keep their animals alive over the winter.)*
FOLLOW-UP: **How does this situation connect to Ma and Pa leaving the girls at home?** *(Possible response: This must be one reason the girls need to be so responsible.)*

page 163

📖 **All the other cattle . . . after them.**

6. To determine that Laura seems able to attack problems while Mary freezes: **What does the way both girls initially react to the problem show us about each?** *(Possible response: Laura aggressively started to shoo away the cattle, which shows us she thinks fast. Mary froze, which shows us that even though she's older, she seems to need Laura around.)*

📖 **More and more hay . . . over it.**

7. To further elucidate the degree of danger and difficulty associated with living on the prairie: **What's the author showing us?** *(Possible response: The author is using these details to show that no matter what Laura, Mary, and Jack do, they can't seem to shoo the cattle away. They always seem to be on the verge of being trampled.)*
FOLLOW-UP: **What does this tell us about prairie life?** *(Possible response: It's dangerous and hard.)*

page 164
📖 **He did not . . . were Norwegian.**

8. To highlight the way one person's irresponsibility can impact another person: **How does Johnny fit into this scene with the cows?** *(Possible response: He should have been watching them instead of sleeping.)*
FOLLOW-UP: **What does this show us about life on the prairie?** *(Possible response: If you don't do your job, you could really affect someone else's life.)*

page 165
📖 **Often he and Laura stood up . . . sitting down.**

9. To establish that the girls have lost all inclination toward fun and adventure: **How do the girls' moods fit with their earlier argument?** *(Possible response: They seem so worn out that all they want is for Ma and Pa to return. They aren't arguing over something as silly as playing on a rock.)*

page 166
📖 **Pa came bounding . . . the goad.**

10. To illustrate that the happy event of Ma and Pa returning has now turned frightening:

What's going on? *(Possible response: The oxen seem to be pulling the wagon way too fast, putting everyone in danger. The girls are scared instead of happy to see the wagon returning.)*

page 167
📖 **Her face was gray . . . all over.**

11. To establish that when this family solves one problem, there seems to be another on the horizon: **How does this scene add to what we know about prairie life?** *(Possible response: Life is hard. One problem is solved and another pops up in its place.)*

📖 **"Now girls, help . . . the oxen."**

12. To further solidify the tenacity of this family: **What do you think of Ma's reaction to what just happened?** *(Possible response: Pretty amazing. Even though frightened, she realized everything was okay and just told everyone to move on to the next chore.)*
FOLLOW-UP: **How does Ma's reaction connect to life on the prairie?** *(Possible response: It just shows there's no time to sit and worry. Move on to the next thing.)*

page 169
📖 **Ma sat just . . . her arms.**

13. To establish that small, simple things are big rewards on the prairie: **What does everyone think of Pa's treat?** *(Possible response: They're ecstatic. It's a big treat to get even a small bit of candy.)*

📖 **It would be . . . wheat crop.**

14. To further highlight that Laura has a mind of her own: **The author writes that Laura was not contradicting; she was only saying what she thought. How does that add to what you know about Laura?** *(Possible response: Laura's a thinker, a person with her own ideas. This often comes off as being stubborn.)*

Justin and the Best Biscuits in the World, pages 186–202

page 188

📖 **When Grandpa invites . . . eager to go.**

1. To set up that Justin is so miserable (feels as though he can do nothing right) at home that he jumps at the chance to stay at his grandfather's ranch: **What has the author told us about Justin's life so far?** *(Possible response: Justin doesn't do chores very well and gets so upset with his home life that his grandfather invites him to stay at his ranch. Justin happily accepts the invitation.)*

page 189

📖 **Justin ate two . . . everything else.**

2. To draw attention to Justin's good mood: **What does Justin's behavior this morning show us about his mood?** *(Possible response: He seems happy, hopping out of bed, eating lots of food.)*

📖 **He waited.**

3. To have students connect Justin's attitude toward the chores Grandpa is doing to the earlier notion that household chores are women's work: **What's going on with Justin now?** *(Possible response: He seems to be struggling with feelings of guilt as Grandpa does all the chores and Justin does nothing.)*
FOLLOW-UP: **How does this situation connect to what we learned about Justin when he was home with his sisters and mother?** *(Possible response: Justin felt sorry for himself because he wasn't good at women's work, and now he's being asked to do the same things at Grandpa's ranch and refusing to do them.)*

page 191

📖 **"Everything's easy when you know how."**

4. To begin to establish the gentle but firm way Grandpa teaches Justin without having to battle with him: **What does this conversation between Grandpa and Justin show us?** *(Possible response: The conversation shows Grandpa expects Justin to do certain things but will teach him what's expected. Justin feels good when he finally does something "chore-like"—folding clothes with the help of his grandfather.)*

page 192

📖 **"I guess that's a joke, eh?" Justin laughed.**

5. To further establish Grandpa's nurturing nature: **Grandpa and Justin holding hands, Grandpa allowing Justin to help him do important jobs, Grandpa's jokes: What does all this show us about Grandpa?** *(Possible response: He seems to really care about Justin.)*

To establish that ranch life is tedious and difficult: **What does the author's description of riding fence show us?** *(Possible response: Life on the ranch isn't easy.)*

page 194

📖 **The baby trotted behind.**

6. To establish that Grandpa and Justin help a fawn out of the sharp wire fence that her head was caught in: **What's going on?** *(Possible response: Justin and Grandpa stopped working so they could untangle a fawn from the sharp wire fence.)*

© Harcourt

page 195

📖 Justin felt better. . . riding fence.

7. To have students understand that the way Grandpa treats Black when he's nervous is similar to the way he treats Justin: **Grandpa told Justin to let Black run when he seemed nervous—not to try to hold him back at that time. How does this connect to the way Grandpa handled Justin when he didn't do chores?** *(Possible response: Grandpa gave Justin some space, didn't force him to do chores, and then, after a time, gently showed Justin the way to take care of his clothes and his room. Grandpa seems to understand you can't push or pull people or horses all the time to get them to go in the right direction.)*

page 197

📖 With his long . . . of dough.

8. To establish that Justin is surprised Grandpa is making their lunch from scratch: **What's going on?** *(Possible response: Grandpa and Justin have stopped at a shed where Grandpa is making lunch from flour and other basic ingredients.)*
FOLLOW-UP: **What does Justin think of Grandpa preparing lunch this way?** *(Possible response: He seems surprised by the whole thing—that Grandpa can do such a thing.)*

📖 "Keep your eyes . . . any snakes."

9. To establish that Grandpa trusts Justin to take care of the horses and that this must make Justin feel good about himself: **What's Grandpa showing us by asking Justin to take the horses to drink?** *(Possible response: Grandpa trusts Justin to stay safe and keep the horses safe.)*
FOLLOW-UP: **What do you suppose Justin thinks about this?** *(Possible response: Justin probably feels good about himself now—thinks maybe he can take care of some chores.)*

page 198

📖 The look he gave Grandpa revealed his doubts.

10. To further connect Justin's earlier thought that certain chores were women's work to Grandpa's talents for performing chores of all kinds: **How does Justin's comment about men and cooking add to what we knew at the beginning of the story?** *(Possible response: Justin seems to think certain activities are for men and others are for women.)*

page 199

📖 Grandpa offered Justin the last biscuit.

11. To establish that Grandpa has shown Justin more surprising facts about the world: **What does Justin's reaction to Grandpa's stories about Black cowboys show us?** *(Possible response: Justin's reaction shows us he had no idea that his grandfather had been a cowboy or that Black people in general were cowboys. He's learning so much from Grandpa.)*

page 201

📖 ". . . What matters is . . . enjoyable way."

12. To establish that Grandpa thinks anyone can perform any job that he/she works hard at learning: **What does this conversation between Grandpa and Justin show us?** *(Possible response: Grandpa believes that the only thing keeping someone from doing a specific type of work is not knowing how to do it.)*

page 202

📖 He wished he . . . loved him.

13. To fully establish the deep connection that has formed between Justin and Grandpa: **"A warmth spread over Justin and he lowered his eyes." What does this sentence tell us?** *(Possible response: Justin realizes that even with all his faults, Grandpa has loved him since the day he was born. Justin is overwhelmed with the feeling of being so loved.)*

Three Little Cyberpigs,
pages 216–223

📖 **WOLF dashes off . . . through curtain.**

1. To set up that this play deals with familiar characters who, so far, are engaged in a familiar conflict: **What has the author set up for us?** *(Possible response: This play is about the Three Little Pigs and the wolf who is chasing them after not being able to blow their brick house down.)*

📖 **Come see the folks in Cyberland.**

2. To establish that the three pigs have entered a cyber-lab where Ann promises to help them: **What's going on with this mouse named Ann?** *(Possible response: She works in a computer lab and promises to help the pigs handle the wolf, who is hot on their trail.)*

📖 **ANN and PIGS applaud.**

3. To focus on the way the author is having the characters from various stories work together: **What's going on with the nursery-rhyme characters?** *(Possible response: The characters from particular stories seem to be working together on the computer instead of causing each other the usual trouble.)*

📖 **And said, ". . . boy am I!"**

4. To have students recognize that the characters are solving their nursery-rhyme problems with computers: **Why are the characters so pleased with the computers in Cyberland?** *(Possible response: They are using the computers to solve the problems they had in the original nursery rhymes.)*

📖 He'll ruin the store; you'll have to quit.

5. To have students use the ideas they've constructed so far to determine that Ann and the other characters will probably use the computers to solve the pigs' problem with the wolf: **Knowing what you do about the story, what do you think Ann will do to save the pigs?** *(Possible response: She will probably show the pigs how to use the computer to get rid of the wolf.)*

📖 Pigs in Cyberland, hooray!

6. To establish that the pigs are satisfied with Ann's services: **How do the pigs react to what Ann has done?** *(Possible response: They're so happy with Ann and Cyberland that they all want computers.)*

Weaving a California Tradition, pages 240–255

page 240
📖 Carly lives with . . . Sierra Nevada Mountains.

1. To establish that Carly Tex is descended from Western Mono basketweavers and that her family still weaves, keeping the tradition alive: **What has the author set up for us?** (Possible response: The author introduced Carly and her family as being basketweavers who have carried on the Western Mono tradition.)

page 242
📖 For example, there . . . Fork Mono.

2. To have students discern that although Carly's family is heavily involved in weaving, they all have other obligations: **How does basketmaking fit into the life of Carly and her family?** (Possible response: They're all involved with making baskets, but they all also have school or other jobs to do.)

page 243
📖 Deergrass has narrow . . . in baskets.

3. To draw attention to the notion that the types of baskets someone weaves is determined by where the person lives: **Why does the author include information about geography and climate when discussing basketweaving?** (Possible response: The kinds of baskets the weavers make depend on the materials available. Certain basket materials only grow in particular areas.)

page 245
📖 They look for . . . different kinds of baskets.

4. To establish that the family happily works together to gather weaving materials at just the right time of year: **How does the family's gathering of materials connect to the seasons?** (Possible response: They must gather certain items in the summer and others in the fall.) FOLLOW-UP: **How does the family seem to feel about this hard work?** (Possible response: They have fun and enjoy the outdoors.)

page 246
📖 Weavers take care . . . what they take.

5. To emphasize the great degree of care for the plants and the earth that's involved in cutting plants for baskets: **How does the gathering of weaving materials help the plants?** (Possible response: The weavers help thin crowded plants and create fewer places for harmful insects to live. The result is new, healthy growth.)

page 247
📖 This way they . . . be forgotten.

6. To further establish the degree to which families maintain their traditions through the hard work of the weaving process: **How do groups of people figure into the weaving process?** (Possible response: When Carly and her family include people who are new to weaving, they are doing a lot to maintain their heritage by passing along the craft.)

© Harcourt

page 249

📖 **Making the cradleboard . . . more sticks.**

7. To draw attention to the intricate work involved in making these baskets: **How would you describe the process involved in making the baskets Carly chose to create?** *(Possible response: The work is hard and intricate, but she seems to enjoy both the process of weaving and then having someone show her ways to make her baskets better.)*

page 251

📖 **It is a day . . . of both.**

8. To further develop the idea that basketweavers not only find satisfaction in creating something but also appreciate that the process allows them to share their heritage: **What does the basketweaver gathering show us about the weavers?** *(Possible response: The weavers enjoy showing off their work, but learning, teaching, and basking in their heritage are as important as creating something wonderful.)*

page 252

📖 **By bedtime, Carly . . . night's sleep.**

9. To elicit that Carly has had a wonderful day: **How did the first day of the gathering go for Carly?** *(Possible response: Carly is proud that she has work to submit to the show and has had a great day with her family, learning and helping.)*

page 254

📖 **The cocoons are . . . wooden handle.**

10. To have students understand that the weavers spend the day showing visitors traditional ways to make instruments: **What's going on?** *(Possible response: The weavers, including Carly, show visitors different things that their ancestors have been making and using for centuries.)*

page 255

📖 **"I want to . . . generations," she says.**

11. To fully establish that Carly understands that learning to weave baskets and passing the tradition on to others is central to her existence: **What has Carly learned from her relatives and from being involved in basketweaving?** *(Possible response: She has seen the way that weaving creates bonds that tie her to her ancestors, and she will do the same for her descendants as she vows to teach her children to weave someday.)*

page 289

📖 **They are adaptations . . . to survive.**

1. To set up that this piece will explore some ways animals/living things use trickery that protects them and helps them survive: **What does one animal/living thing "tricking" another have to do with camouflage and mimicry?** *(Possible response: Camouflage and mimicry are traits some living things use that deceive or trick their enemies so they can survive in nature.)*

page 290

📖 **If a polar . . . snow and ice.**

2. To have students recognize that color is central to an animal's ability to camouflage itself: **How does color help both predators and prey?** *(Possible response: The right colors keep certain animals from being seen by those who are hunting them. The right colors also allow predators to hide in their environment and surprise unsuspecting prey. Both are examples of animals benefiting from camouflage.)*

page 293

📖 **Some leaf beetles look like caterpillar droppings.**

3. To establish that camouflage can mean an organism can hide, not just by blending in color-wise, but by looking like something that isn't appealing to its predators: **How do pebble plants and katydids connect to this idea of camouflage?** *(Possible response: Both organisms can hide from predators because they look like something that would be inedible to their*

predators. Their camouflage is that they look like rocks, leaves, or sticks.)*

page 294

📖 **A plant or . . . Batesian mimic.**

4. To begin to explore the way mimicry connects to camouflage in that it helps animals survive, but in a different way: **How does Batesian mimicry connect to camouflage?** *(Possible response: Like camouflage, Batesian mimicry helps animals survive by tricking, but it does so by allowing one animal to copy the way a more deadly animal looks so it can scare off predators. Because predators have learned to stay away from the more deadly animal, when they see something with similar markings, they stay away from it, too.)*

page 295

📖 **Because birds get . . . tasted bad.**

5. To further develop the way mimicry protects animals: **How does Müllerian mimicry protect animals?** *(Possible response: This type of mimicry packs a double whammy—the markings mirror those of deadly animals, but the animal "borrowing" the markings is harmful in its own right. This further helps discourage predators from sampling prey bearing particular markings.)*

page 297

📖 **When an insect . . . meal instead.**

6. To establish that some animals have body parts that allow them to trick their prey into coming close enough to easily eat: **How do worm-like tongues, fins that look like worms,**

and bright flowers connect to mimicry? *(Possible response: These are examples of ways certain animals use their own bodies to trick and attract unsuspecting prey by mimicking something— like worms or bright flowers—that appeals to their prey.)*

pages 298–299

📖 **As the insects . . . dead bodies.**

7. To explore the way animals mimic odors to lure their prey and how that adds to what we know about mimicry so far: **How do odors fit into the world of mimicry?** *(Possible response: Some animals give off scents that are attractive to their prey, luring them in for the kill.)*

📖 **But instead of . . . Photuris female.**

8. To have students recognize that *Photuris* fireflies use flashing patterns that mimic the mating flashes of smaller species to lure their prey: **How do flashing patterns fit into the idea of mimicry?** *(Possible response: Female fireflies flash mating patterns to lure the males of a different species, which then become the female's prey.)*

📖 **Like a hand . . . around them.**

9. To fully establish that camouflage and mimicry are perfectly suited to the animals who use them: **How does the idea of a hand in a glove connect to mimicry and camouflage?** *(Possible response: The author uses this simile to sum up the notion that camouflage and mimicry provide protection or attraction in the exact way a particular animal needs it to—just as the shape of a glove fits the hand perfectly.)*

Mountains, pages 316–329

page 318

📖 **Mountains are born . . . they came.**

1. To draw attention to the notion that mountains seem permanent, but they're always changing: **What has the author set up for us so far?** *(Possible response: The author is bringing up the idea that mountains are always changing even if we can't see the change on a day-to-day basis.)*

📖 **Mountains are tall . . . a mountain?**

2. To begin to establish the criteria that allow us to use the word *mountain* to describe land: **How do the measurements given connect to the author's question about labeling something a mountain?** *(Possible response: Maybe mountains have to be at least 26,000 ft. high to be called a mountain.)*

page 319

📖 **Whether to call . . . surroundings are.**

3. To further establish the murky criteria for calling a landmass a mountain: **How does the information about the Alps, Andes, etc., help characterize something as a mountain?** *(Possible response: This information makes it even less clear.)*
FOLLOW-UP: **What does the author mean that defining something as a mountain depends on who is looking at it and how high its surroundings are?** *(Possible response: Mountain height seems to be relative to what's around it.)*

page 320

📖 **The islands of . . . Mid-Atlantic ridge.**

4. To establish that mountains are formed where plates in the earth are located and come about when the plates push and pull: **What do plates have to do with the formation of mountain ranges?** *(Possible response: When the earth's plates pull apart in one place they push together in another place; land folds upward, creating ranges of higher elevations: mountains.)*

page 322

📖 **When the bare . . . in Montana.**

5. To draw attention to the surprising nature of rock—its obviously strong, resilient characteristics combined with the ability to fold and shift: **What's the author trying to show with the paper example?** *(Possible response: The author suggests this experiment as a way to show the way land folds and creates mountains when plates push and pull.)*
FOLLOW-UP: **What does this show us about the rocks that make up mountain ranges?** *(Possible response: Rocks are surprisingly bendable when slow, strong pressure is applied.)*

page 323

📖 **The Sierra Nevada . . . fault-block mountains.**

6. To establish that mountain ranges are also formed where the earth's plates pull apart: **How does the idea of fault blocks connect to the formation of mountains?** *(Possible response: The earth's plates separate, providing an opportunity for rocks to shift, rise, or fall, creating mountains.)* To have students discern that both ends of

© Harcourt

a plate system are affected when they shift: **How does the process of mountains forming when plates pull apart connect to mountains forming when plates push together?** (*Possible response: It shows that both ends of the plates are affected when the earth shifts.*)

page 325
📖 **Yosemite's Half Dome . . . years ago.**

7. To have students determine that the creation of dome mountains and volcanic mountains are further examples of the ways mountains form: **How do volcanic and dome mountains connect to what we know about folded and fault-block mountains?** (*Possible response: Volcanic and dome mountains are also formed when parts of the earth change.*)

page 327
📖 **The material that . . . move downhill.**

8. To examine the way weathering and erosion change the shape of mountains: **How is moisture and weather a part of mountain formation/change?** (*Possible response: Water in the form of rain, rivers, and glaciers rubs and beats against mountains, carving out and tearing parts from the surface. Cold temperatures freeze and warm temperatures thaw moisture, causing it to create cracks and break off pieces of rock.*)

page 328
📖 **When air is . . . fog, and rain.**

9. To establish the way mountain ranges affect moisture in their surrounding areas: **How are rain, fog, mist, and cloud cover related to mountain ranges?** (*Possible response: Mountains force air to climb up and over them. The air cools as it rises and its water vapor condenses in the form of fog, mist, clouds, and rain.*)

📖 **Clouds form and . . . western slopes.**

10. To connect the climate associated with the Pacific Northwest to the mountains nearby: **How does the notion that mountains affect climate connect to the weather we'd see in the Pacific coastal mountain ranges?** (*Possible response: The author tells us that wet winds blow off the ocean. They must climb up the sides of mountains, cooling and releasing their moisture as rain. The western slopes of Pacific mountain ranges are so wet that they qualify as rain forests.*)

page 329
📖 **The driest deserts . . . few hundred miles.**

11. To clarify that the air that climbs the western side of the Pacific mountain ranges must drop most of its moisture before it reaches the eastern slopes: **How is it possible that the driest deserts in America and the wettest rain forests are separated by only a few hundred miles?** (*Possible response: As the air comes up the rain-forest side of the mountains, it must drop all of its moisture, leaving the eastern side dry as the air passes over it.*)

📖 **Mountains offer a chance . . . in the world.**

12. To highlight the numerous ways mountains provide important resources for everyday life: **What's the author showing us now?** (*Possible response: Mountains provide water, fertile areas, and fun for people who live there.*)

Fire Storm, pages 344–354

page 346
📖 **He had only dumped twice!**

1. To have students recognize that Axel has earned this trip to the wilderness by achieving good grades in history—a subject he dislikes: **What's the author letting us know about Axel's life?** *(Possible response: Axel is visiting his aunt and uncle, having a great summer. They are rewarding him for earning good grades in a subject he dislikes.)*

page 348
📖 **"That fire is . . . the mountain."**

2. To have students ascertain that even though Axel is a boy, he's a skilled kayaker: **What has the author shown us about the way Axel handles his kayak?** *(Possible response: The way he maneuvers his kayak over waterfalls and around boulders all by himself shows he's very good at kayaking.)* To have students recognize the out-of-the-way setting in which this story takes place: **What do the author's details about the setting let us know about the story?** *(Possible response: Axel, Aunt Charlotte, and Uncle Paul are out in the middle of nowhere— with nothing but nature and animals.)*

📖 **He kept watching the fires.**

3. To establish that the fires that were once far away are now very close: **What's happening with the fires?** *(Possible response: The fires that were once far away from the river are now threatening Alex and his aunt and uncle.)* To draw attention to the way fire has changed the mood of the trip: **Why is Uncle Paul refusing to unpack the camping gear?**

(Possible response: Even though he said the fire won't burn on their side of the river, he must still be a little worried that it will.)

page 350
📖 **Axel tied one . . . was fresher.**

4. To have students understand that the fire has grown into a fire storm, eating up everything in sight, and that the answer to what to do next is not totally clear: **What's happening with the fire now?** *(Possible response: It's growing more powerful and dangerous by the minute.)* FOLLOW-UP: **What does Uncle Paul mean when he says, "It's better to sit still in the known than plunge into the unknown"?** *(Possible response: They need to weigh the best way to proceed carefully, since the fire seems more and more unpredictable.)*

page 352
📖 **It was an inferno of flames.**

5. To accentuate how smart Axel and his uncle are: **What do the ideas Axel has contributed show us about him?** *(Possible response: He seems really smart.)* FOLLOW-UP: **How do Axel's ideas connect to Uncle Paul's saying a solution would present itself?** *(Possible response: Axel waited calmly, observing aspects of the fire before making suggestions—the solution to go to the burnt-out campground presented itself to Axel.)*

📖 "I want to cry . . . lost forest."

6. To establish that Axel feels very connected to the wilderness and saddened by what the fire has done: **Why is Axel almost to the point of tears now?** (*Possible response: He's sad that the forest has been obliterated.*)
FOLLOW-UP: **How does this add to what we know about the way he feels about how he's spending his summer?** (*Possible response: He seems in love with everything in nature and with kayaking—his sadness further shows how much he loves his surroundings.*)

📖 "I'll see you . . ." he said, and smiled.

7. To have students understand the connection between Aunt Charlotte's phoenix story and the burnt forest: **How does Aunt Charlotte's story connect to Axel's concern about the burnt-out forest?** (*Possible response: The story of the phoenix shows that life does regenerate itself from the bits and pieces that might not be noticeable to the casual onlooker.*)
FOLLOW-UP: **What does Axel mean when he says to the eagle that he'll see him next summer?** (*Possible response: He's referring to his uncle's information about coming back in a year, when the forest will have regenerated itself.*)

page 372

📖 He got up . . . the truck.

1. To establish that on an ordinary "almost" fall day, Farmer Bailey hit a man with his truck: **What has the author set up for us?** *(Possible response: Farmer Bailey was thinking about how much he enjoyed the almost-fall weather when he accidentally hit a man with his truck.)*

page 374

📖 "I don't think . . . to talk."

2. To have students discern that the stranger seems dazed and unable to talk: **What does the conversation between Mr. and Mrs. Bailey show us about the stranger?** *(Possible response: The man can't speak, and Mr. Bailey thinks he might be a person who lives alone, far from other people—a hermit.)*
FOLLOW-UP: **How might the stranger's silence connect to the accident?** *(Possible response: Maybe he hit his head and can't remember how to talk.)*

page 375

📖 "It's broken, the . . . the bottom.

3. To draw attention to the thermometer breaking: **What's going on with the thermometer?** *(Possible response: Somehow it broke and all the mercury slid to one end of it.)*

page 376

📖 "There's a draft in here tonight."

4. To establish that the stranger's inability to function seems beyond the doctor's diagnosis: **How does the man's behavior connect to the doctor's diagnosis?** *(Possible response: The doctor said the man lost his memory, but not knowing how to eat soup seems even more drastic than not remembering who you are.)*
To highlight the connection between the stranger blowing on his soup and the cool draft: **Why does Mrs. Bailey comment on the room being drafty?** *(Possible response: It seems as though when the stranger blew on his soup it caused a cool breeze.)*

page 377

📖 The rabbits hopped . . . to follow.

5. To draw attention to the odd way the rabbits took to the stranger: **What's going on?** *(Possible response: The stranger seems to have an unusual connection to animals.)*

📖 But the stranger . . . even sweat.

6. To begin to piece together the idea that the stranger seems otherworldly: **How does the stranger's untiring work connect to everything we've learned about him so far?** *(Possible response: He seems to have some kind of supernatural powers.)*

📖 **"It's hard to believe he's a hermit."**

7. To establish that Mr. Bailey still seems to think the stranger is a hermit and that he's surprised a hermit would enjoy his family so much: **What does Mr. Bailey mean when he says "It's hard to believe he's a hermit"?** *(Possible response: Mr. Bailey is still under the impression the stranger is a hermit, but the stranger likes to be with the family–the opposite of what a hermit might enjoy.)*

📖 **The leaves on . . . weeks before.**

8. To establish that the odd weather pattern coincides with the accident and with the unusual person the stranger seems to be: **How do Mr. Bailey's observations about the weather connect to the accident with the stranger?** *(Possible response: Three weeks ago was when the accident occurred and when the weather seemed to become stuck in "almost" fall.)*

FOLLOW-UP: **How might the unusual weather connect to the unusual qualities of the stranger?** *(Possible response: He seems to be unusually tuned into nature, so maybe he has something to do with the weather pattern.)*

📖 **He held it . . . with all his might.**

9. To have students connect the stranger's sense about the trees to his past unusual acts: **How does the stranger's latest interaction with nature (looking at the trees) connect to what we know about him already?**

(Possible response: Just as when he connected with the rabbits and was mesmerized by the birds, he seems to sense something about the trees and the way the leaves should long ago have turned colors.)

📖 **The air had . . . longer green.**

10. To establish the connection between the stranger and temperature/weather changes: **What's happening with the stranger now?** *(Possible response: The stranger made an abrupt exit.)*

FOLLOW-UP: **How does the stranger connect to the temperature and local weather?** *(Possible response: The stranger seems to have a chilling effect on things—the thermometer breaking, the draft at dinner, and the weather turning cold upon his exit.)*

📖 **"See you next fall."**

11. To have students determine the stranger returns each year with cold weather and stunning fall colors: **What's going on?** *(Possible response: It seems as though the stranger returns every year, bringing the area surrounding the farm its fall temperatures, colors, etc.)* To have students entertain the idea that the man might be Jack Frost: **How does this story connect to the "man" we call Jack Frost?** *(Possible response: Perhaps this is the story of Jack Frost and the way he makes his way around the world, bringing different areas from summer into fall.)*

page 416

📖 And you want . . . inventor, too?

1. To clarify that this text deals with inventions: **What has the author told us so far?** (Possible response: She listed several inventions we use every day—the text must be about inventions.)

page 417

📖 (He probably needed them!)

2. To establish that inventors can be any age: **What have we learned about inventors so far?** (Possible response: Inventors can be young or old and still create important things.)

FOLLOW-UP: **How does Benjamin Franklin fit with the idea that age isn't a factor when inventing?** (Possible response: He proves that age doesn't matter—he invented simple paddles as a child and sophisticated things like bifocals as an older man.)

page 418

📖 But they wanted . . . or nothing!

3. To emphasize that inventors observe ways in which everyday work is hard and then find ways to make it easier: **What did the author mean when she said, "If you want to be an inventor, find a need and fill it"?** (Possible response: Both McCormick and McCoy created items that made their work much easier and faster.)

FOLLOW-UP: **What's all this about "the real McCoy"?** (Possible response: People thought Elijah McCoy's lubricator was the best one available and wouldn't settle for an imitation.)

page 419

📖 With its three blades . . . took off.

4. To establish that inventors were often inspired by dreams that came true through hard work: **How are these inventors and the idea of dreams connected?** (Possible response: They often dreamed about things that others laughed at, but with hard work their dreams turned to reality.)

📖 Velcro!

5. To clarify that inventors often take their ideas from nature or things other people are already doing: **How does "keeping your eyes open" fit with being an inventor?** (Possible response: In each case the inventor saw something happen and took the event as a jumping-off point for his invention.)

page 420

📖 Thanks to "Moon Man" . . . spacecraft *Apollo 11* landed Americans safely on the moon in 1969.

6. To further emphasize the element of perseverance in creating successful inventions: **From what you read, what can you say about the kind of people these inventors were?** (Possible response: They all worked hard, even in the face of obstacles beyond their control, and in the end became successful because of their persistence.)

© Harcourt